W9-BYJ-664

MONUMENTAL MILESTONES
GREAT EVENTS OF MODERN TIMES

The Watergate Scandal

Richard Nixon's involvement in the cover-up surrounding a break-in at Democratic National Committee headquarters in the Watergate Complex began a scandal that rocked the White House, and the American public.

Mitchell Lane
PUBLISHERS

P.O. Box 196
Hockessin, Delaware 19707

Titles in the Series

MONUMENTAL MILESTONES
GREAT EVENTS OF MODERN TIMES

The
Watergate
Scandal

In this political cartoon from June 26, 1973, Richard Nixon is being washed away by the flood of wrongdoings committed by him and his administration.

Kathleen Tracy

Copyright © 2007 by Mitchell Lane Publishers, Inc. All rights reserved. No part of this book may be reproduced without written permission from the publisher. Printed and bound in the United States of America.

Printing   1   2   3   4   5   6   7   8   9

Library of Congress Cataloging-in-Publication Data
Tracy, Kathleen.
   The Watergate Scandal / by Kathleen Tracy.
       p. cm. — (Monumental milestones)
   Includes bibliographical references and index.
   ISBN 1-58415-470-5 (library bound : alk. paper)
   1. Watergate Affair, 1972–1974—Juvenile literature. 2. Nixon, Richard, M. (Richard Milhous), 1913—Juvenile literature. 3. United States—Politics and government—1969–1974—Juvenile literature. I. Title. II. Series.
   E860.T72 2006
   973.924—dc22   2005028507

ISBN-10: 1-58415-470-5   ISBN-13: 978-1-58415-470-9

ABOUT THE AUTHOR: Kathleen Tracy has been a journalist for over twenty years. Her writing has been featured in magazines including *The Toronto Star*'s "Star Week," *A Biography* magazine, *KidScreen* and *TV Times*. She is also the author of numerous biographies and other nonfiction books, including *Mariano Guadalupe Vallejo, William Hewlett: Pioneer of the Computer Age, The Fall of the Berlin Wall*, and *Top Secret: The Manhattan Project* for Mitchell Lane Publishers.

PHOTO CREDITS: Front cover—Bill Pierce/Time Life Pictures/Getty Images; pp. 1, 28—Ford Library Museum; pp. 3, 12, 17, 18, 26, 36, 40—Library of Congress; p. 6—Hulton Archive/Getty Images; p. 14—*Life*; p. 15—*Reader Weekly*; p. 31—Corbis; p. 34—Stennis Center.

PUBLISHER'S NOTE: This story is based on the author's extensive research, which she believes to be accurate. Documentation of such research is contained on page 47.

The internet sites referenced herein were active as of the publication date. Due to the fleeting nature of some web sites, we cannot guarantee they will all be active when you are reading this book.

Contents

The Watergate Scandal

Kathleen Tracy

*For Your Information

Located along the banks of the Potomac River, the Watergate is a huge complex of apartments, office buildings, shops, and a luxury hotel.

Because of its central location, many government organizations have had offices at the Watergate, including the Democratic National Committee. The name Watergate would become synonymous with government conspiracy after the scandal implicated top members of the White House staff—and the President himself.

In the Dead of the Night

Nestled alongside the Potomac River in Washington, D.C., is the sprawling Watergate Complex. Opened in 1967, the site is comprised of three apartment buildings, a shopping center, two office buildings, and the luxurious Watergate Hotel. Because of its central location in the city, many political organizations have rented office space there. In 1972, the Democratic National Committee, or DNC, had its headquarters at the Watergate. The DNC is the primary fund-raising organization for the Democratic Party.

On Sunday, May 28, 1972, a team of men working under the cover of darkness broke into the DNC's suite of offices. They were not burglars in the normal sense, because their intention was not to just steal. Their primary mission was to install bugs, or wiretaps, inside the office of committee chairman Lawrence F. O'Brien in order to eavesdrop on O'Brien's phone calls and office conversations, as well as to monitor the activities of the DNC.

Across the street, in room 723 of a Howard Johnson's Motor Lodge, the spies spent the next several weeks listening to the wiretaps, hoping to find out what individuals were contributing money to the Democrats and any other useful information they could pick up concerning the upcoming presidential election. When one of the wiretaps failed, a second mission was ordered. In the afternoon of June 16, one of the burglars, James W. McCord, posed as a delivery man, and while in the building he taped the locks of stairwell doors up to the sixth floor, where the DNC's

offices were located. That accomplished, McCord and the others waited for night to fall. . . .

It had been a typical quiet night when twenty-four-year-old security guard Frank Wills arrived for his midnight shift. Around 1:00 A.M. on June 17, while making his rounds, he noticed some tape on one of the stairwell doors. He discovered that the lock had been taped, which prevented the door from automatically locking when shut. When he found several other doors similarly taped, Wills assumed the cleaning crew was responsible; they often taped the locks or jammed them with paper so that they could easily go from floor to floor when cleaning after hours. But the crew was long gone. Wills removed the tape, made sure the doors were locked, and walked to the Howard Johnson's to grab a cheeseburger. . . .

When McCord and his four accomplices showed up at the Watergate to replace the malfunctioning bug, they discovered the doors were locked. Instead of calling off the mission, McCord chose to continue. He picked the locks and retaped them as the burglars made their way to the DNC offices. . . .

After Wills returned from his dinner break, he again went on his rounds—and again discovered the stairwell door locks had been jammed. Now he knew for certain this had nothing to do with the cleaning crew. He immediately called his supervisor and the police.

The call came into the Washington, D.C., dispatch at 1:52 A.M. A team of three detectives from the tactical squad were sent to the scene. They followed the trail of taped doors from the basement of the building to the sixth floor, where they found the door to the Democratic National Committee had been jimmied. With guns drawn, they entered the suite of twenty-nine offices and searched the rooms one by one. Suddenly, a man jumped up from behind a desk, arms raised over his head, and in a panicked voice pleaded, "Don't shoot!"[1]

As more information came to light over the course of the day, the thwarted burglary had journalists and politicians alike buzzing. Police

had apprehended five men, all wearing surgical gloves; $2,300 in hundred-dollar bills, with the serial numbers in sequence; a bag of sophisticated bugging and burglary equipment; and documents related to strategies for the upcoming national election.

The election committee for U.S. President Richard Nixon denied knowledge of wiretapping, and the White House declined comment, but DNC's chief Larry O'Brien was outraged, saying the break-in "raised the ugliest questions about the integrity of the political process that I have encountered in a quarter century. No mere statement of innocence by Mr. Nixon's campaign manager will dispel these questions."[2]

Initially, the five burglars gave police false names, but eventually their true identities were established—and that's when some began to suspect the Watergate break-in was not merely a random act committed by overzealous Nixon supporters as the White House tried to intimate. The men were Bernard Barker, a former CIA operative who worked in real estate in Miami; Virgilio Gonzales, a Cuban refugee; Eugenio Martinez, an employee of Barker's who was also from Cuba; Frank Sturgis, known to have CIA connections; and the group's leader, James McCord, a security adviser for the Republican National Committee and the Committee for the Re-election of the President, amusingly known as CREEP. McCord, whose real name was Edward Martin, was also a former FBI and CIA agent.

When news of McCord's involvement was released, John Mitchell, the head of CREEP, acknowledged McCord had been contracted to provide security services but stressed to *The Washington Post* that the burglars "were not operating either in our behalf or with our consent. . . . There is no place in our campaign, or in the electoral process, for this type of activity and we will not permit it nor condone it."[3]

Senator Bob Dole, then Republican National Committee chairman, added, "We deplore action of this kind in or out of politics. . . . If our understanding of the facts is accurate we will of course discontinue our relationship with the firm."[4]

Curiously, neither Mitchell nor Dole nor anyone else in the Republican National Committee knew exactly who had hired McCord, when he had been hired, how much he was being paid, or what his responsibilities were. Also surprising were the high-powered defense lawyers taking the burglars' case—men with apparently limited means.

In hindsight, it seems obvious that McCord's involvement indicated that persons higher in the Nixon administration must have known about his activities. But in 1972, most people felt there was no reason *not* to believe the government. When Nixon spokespeople denied any involvement, the majority of Americans, including members of the press, were willing to believe them. As a result, in November that year, Richard Nixon defeated George McGovern by a landslide. After such a lopsided victory, many in Nixon's White House believed the Watergate incident would eventually blow over.

And it might have, except for two dogged journalists from *The Washington Post*. Their names were Carl Bernstein and Bob Woodward. With the support of their editor, Ben Bradlee, the reporters would end up devoting their professional and personal lives to the story for the next year. In the end they unraveled one of the greatest political mysteries and exposed one of the greatest presidential scandals in United States history.

FYInfo
For Your Information

Frank Wills

Frank Wills was simply doing his job the night his discovery of taped door locks led to the apprehension of the Watergate burglars. But soon he was being presented as a hero in the news media. It was a David and Goliath story—an $80-a-week security guard was alert enough to foil a sophisticated band of suspects. So many reporters wanted to interview Wills that he hired a lawyer/agent and charged a $300 fee for his time, which a few actually paid.

As more and more people in the Nixon White House became implicated in the burglary, others began to recognize the importance of Wills's contribution. The Democratic Party honored him, and he received the Martin Luther King Award from the Southern Christian Leadership Conference. He was even asked to play himself in the movie about Watergate, *All the President's Men,* starring Robert Redford and Dustin Hoffman.

Wills quickly learned there was a downside to sudden fame—that it can be over just as suddenly. His plan to tour the country speaking about the break-in fizzled when nobody was interested in booking his services. He quit his job with the security firm at the Watergate Hotel in a reported dispute over their refusal to offer paid vacation days. In 1973, he complained to *The Washington Post* that he was having trouble finding another job with any other security company. "I don't know if they are being told not to hire me or if they are just afraid to hire me,"[5] he said.

Convinced he was being blacklisted by people afraid of Nixon, Wills eventually left Washington, D.C., to live with his ailing mother in Georgia. In 1983, he was convicted of shoplifting a pair of tennis shoes and sentenced to a year in jail, even though he claimed it had been a misunderstanding.

While taking care of his ailing mother, they scraped by on her $450-a-month Social Security check. Wills grew bitter as many of the men convicted of crimes related to Watergate served short prison sentences. He also resented all those who got rich from book deals. When his mother died, Wills was forced to donate her body to science because he couldn't afford a burial. He was living in a shack without electricity or running water.

On the twenty-fifth anniversary of the Watergate break-in, Wills expressed his bitterness in an interview with the *Boston Globe.* "I was doing what I was supposed to do. I was doing my job. And I caught pure hell. . . . I put my life on the line. If it wasn't for me, Woodward and Bernstein would not have known anything about Watergate. This wasn't finding a dollar under a couch somewhere.

"I never got no kind of commendation. Nobody invited me to the White House. It will be on my mind until the day I close my eyes."[6]

Wills died of a brain tumor in 2000. He was just fifty-two years old.

Richard Milhous Nixon was America's 37th President. Nixon had lost to John F. Kennedy in 1960 in one of the closest elections ever.

When Nixon ran again in 1968, it was assumed Democratic front-runner Robert Kennedy would be in the race against Nixon. But in June of that year, Kennedy was assassinated, forcing the Democratic Party to nominate Hubert Humphrey. Nixon won. Four years later he defeated George McGovern in a landslide.

The Seeds of Paranoia

The early 1970s were an uneasy time in America. An increasingly unpopular war was raging in Vietnam. Racial tensions simmered as the civil rights movement continued to break down color barriers. The 1968 assassinations of Martin Luther King and Robert Kennedy had taken an emotional toll on many citizens. The cultural revolution that had begun in the mid-1960s continued to polarize Americans. On one side were people who trusted government completely and supported the war in Vietnam. On the other side were those, including huge numbers of young people ever more mistrustful of government, who thought Americans were being lied to and demanded that the war be stopped.

In 1968, Richard Nixon had been elected president based in part on his promise of having a "secret plan" to stop the war while maintaining American honor. Also, the expected Democratic nominee, Robert Kennedy, had been assassinated that June, almost ensuring Nixon's victory.

In March 1969, while Americans were given the impression that U.S. involvement in the war was winding down, Nixon began secretly bombing Cambodia, the country located to the west of Vietnam, in an effort to destroy routes used to bring supplies to the North Vietnamese. Neither the public nor even Congress knew of the bombings, called Operation Breakfast.

A month later, *The New York Times* broke the story about the covert bombing. Nixon's response was to have the phones of four journalists and over a dozen government employees wiretapped in an effort

to find out how the *Times* had gotten the information. Despite the story, the raids would continue for over a year. It is estimated that at least 150,000 Cambodian civilians died as a result.

On June 27, *Life* magazine ran photographs of the 242 U.S. soldiers who had been killed the previous week in Vietnam. It is one thing to read numbers; when the public actually saw the faces of young men killed, it increased antiwar sentiment and had more people openly questioning Nixon's policies.

In November 1969, Americans were appalled to learn of the My Lai massacre. U.S. troops searching for Viet Cong soldiers and their sympathizers murdered up to 504 Vietnamese civilians, mostly women and children, in My Lai village. Many of the victims were raped and tortured before being killed. Suddenly, even people who had supported the war began to have doubts about the value of America's involvement.

These are just 12 of the 242 United States soldiers killed in one week in Vietnam.

By 1968, colleges across the country were filled with students protesting the Vietnam war. On June 27, 1969, when Life *magazine printed the pictures of all 242 soldiers killed the previous week, even more conservative Americans began questioning their support of the war.*

During his testimony, Calley claimed he was simply following orders from his superior. Calley was convicted of murder and sentenced to life in prison. He was released in 1974 following years of appeals.

Americans were horrified by the images of the massacre at My Lai. Eventually Lt. William Calley faced court-martial.

On April 30, 1970, Nixon went on television to announce that American troops had invaded Cambodia in search of Viet Cong soldiers. The broadcast created outrage among opponents of the war. Instead of extricating America from Southeast Asia, Nixon seemed to be expanding the conflict. Antiwar protests on college campuses across the nation increased overnight, as did the tension between students and authorities. The shooting deaths of four unarmed Kent State University students by National Guard troops on May 4 shocked the nation but did little to bridge the country's deep political divisions. The antiwar movement continued to grow, as did the government's effort to minimize their impact on public opinion.

Feeling pressured by growing unrest over the war, Nixon was irate when on June 13, 1971, *The New York Times* published the first of a long series of planned articles about a secret government study on the

Vietnam War dubbed the Pentagon Papers. The articles were highly embarrassing to the Nixon administration because they outlined in detail—dating back to the Kennedy administration—how the government had deceived the American public concerning its activities in Southeast Asia and the war. Specifically, they detailed U.S. air strikes in Laos, a supposed neutral country; and they revealed the government's acknowledgment that it was unlikely the war could be won and that the conflict would lead to many more casualties—both of soldiers and civilians—than ever admitted to the American public. More troubling was that the report painted a picture of leaders unconcerned with the loss of life it detailed.

The Nixon administration went to court in hopes of stopping the articles from being published, claiming the Pentagon Papers were classified and publication would harm national security. Meanwhile, on June 18, *The Washington Post* also began publishing the papers. After weeks of legal wrangling, the case ended up in the Supreme Court. On June 30, the Supreme Court ruled 6-3 in favor of *The New York Times* and *The Washington Post,* saying the government could not block publication of the Pentagon Papers. It was a resounding victory for the press and the First Amendment. Nixon was furious; he was determined to ensure such a damaging leak would never happen again. He began plotting against his perceived enemies both inside and outside of government. His paranoia, or belief that people were out to get him, would sow the seeds for his eventual downfall.

Even though he held one of the most powerful positions in the world, President of the United States, Nixon was a man riddled with insecurities. Prior to his election in 1968, he had suffered through two humiliating defeats that would have ended the political career of anyone with less ambition. In 1960, the first ever televised debates between presidential candidates was broadcast. Many people felt Nixon's physical appearance—scrawny, pale, with a five o'clock shadow—helped the robust, tanned John F. Kennedy solidify his lead and win the election.

In 1962 Nixon ran for governor of California but was resound-
ingly defeated by Pat Brown. After blasting the press in his concession
speech, essentially blaming media bias for his loss, Nixon bitterly told
the assembled reporters, "You won't have Nixon to kick around any-
more, because, gentlemen, this is my last press conference."[1] And in
fact, he left California, moved to New York, and went into private legal
practice—for a while.

The lure of public office, with its inherent power, was too great,
and within four years Nixon returned to politics. Two years later he had
managed to win the Republican nomination for president. Many historians believe that had Robert Kennedy—who had won all the major pri-
maries, including California—not been murdered, Nixon would have
suffered yet another crushing political blow. As it was, the eventual

*Richard Nixon's
obsession with
power and
control over
perceived
enemies during
his presidency
had its roots in
these two
crushing political
defeats earlier in
his career.*

Nixon was defeated by John F. Kennedy
(center) in 1960, for president, and Pat
Brown (right) in 1962, for governor.

Hubert Humphrey was vice president under Lyndon Johnson.

After Robert Kennedy's assassination, Humphrey was nominated as the Democratic candidate for the 1968 election.

Democratic candidate, Hubert Humphrey, lost the election by only half a million votes.

As the end of his first term approached, Nixon became increasingly worried about his political opponents who might work against him in the next presidential election. The release of the Pentagon Papers only cemented his mistrust and resentment of the press. Rather than acknowledge he had lied to the public about U.S. policies in Vietnam, he chose to blame the messenger for revealing the lie.

In response to the Pentagon Papers, on July 24, 1971, Nixon formed the ultrasecret Special Investigation Unit. Known by members as the Plumbers, their official job was to prevent any more "leaks" of confidential or sensitive information to the press. In reality, the Plumbers would become Nixon's personal "dirty tricks" squad, whose primary objective was to neutralize the president's enemies—real or perceived.

It was a crime that stunned and embarrassed a nation; it was a trial that divided Americans over what is acceptable use of force in the heat of war; it was an incident that turned the perception of U.S. soldiers in Vietnam from heroes to loose cannons; it was an atrocity that came very close to being successfully covered up.

The events at My Lai (MEE lie) on March 16, 1968, are one of the great tragedies of the war in Vietnam. On that day, soldiers from Charlie Company, 11th Brigade, Americal Division, entered the South Vietnamese village of My Lai in search of enemy fighters from the communist North, as well as any civilian sympathizers.

Morale among the ground troops, who sensed they were fighting a losing battle, was low. In the preceding weeks, several members of Charlie Company had been killed or maimed by mines in the area, so tension—and fear—was running high among the young men. Leading the troops into My Lai was Lieutenant William Calley, who was expecting to engage in a firefight with enemy soldiers. Instead, they found mostly women, children, and elderly members of the village. It would later be reported that these civilians were unarmed.

What happened next is not in dispute. The soldiers gathered the villagers and systematically killed them. Lieutenant Calley himself rounded up a group of 60 that included infants and toddlers, led them to a ditch, and killed them with his machine gun after two other soldiers refused. There were also later eyewitness reports of people being bayoneted, and of some young girls being raped before being shot. Over the course of three hours, up to 504 villagers died as the village was systematically destroyed. Not a single shot had ever been fired at the American soldiers, nor had any enemy soldiers been apprehended or even seen.

When news of the horror reached those higher in command, an immediate cease-fire was ordered—along with efforts to make sure nobody in the United States ever found out. For a year nobody did, until a former soldier named Ron Ridenhour wrote letters to members of Congress about the massacre. In September 1969, William Calley was charged with several counts of premeditated murder. Twenty-five others would eventually also be charged with related crimes. Still, the charges were not made public.

That changed when investigative journalist Seymour Hersh broke the story on November 12. After the Cleveland *Plain Dealer* published photographs of the dead bodies, the military had no choice but to acknowledge the incident and go public.

At the trial, Calley claimed he had been acting under orders from his superior. The superior denied ever giving the order to search and destroy. After the longest court-martial in American history, Calley was convicted in 1971 of premeditated murder and sentenced to life imprisonment. Just two days later, President Nixon ordered him released from prison. Calley ended up serving three and a half years under house arrest at Fort Benning, then was freed.

Former FBI agent G. Gordon Liddy was a member of Nixon's Special Investigation Unit, known as the Plumbers, and helped plan the Watergate break-in.

Liddy was convicted of burglary and contempt of court for refusing to cooperate and answer questions. After spending four years in prison, Liddy was released. He used his Watergate notoriety to land a job hosting a conservative political radio talk show.

C
H
A
P
T
E
R

3

Accusations

One of the first jobs for the Plumbers was to try to publicly discredit the man responsible for leaking the Pentagon Papers, a former State Department military analyst named Daniel Ellsberg. Ellsberg's motivation for photocopying the documents was simply one of conscience. He was shocked at the deception being perpetrated by the government regarding the war and felt Americans should know the truth. Still, it took a while for the truth to come out.

He had actually copied the Pentagon Papers in 1969 and turned the documents over to several senators, but none was willing to release the papers to the public. Only then did he go to *The New York Times, The Washington Post,* and seventeen other newspapers in 1971—even though he believed he would probably spend the rest of his life in jail for doing so.

A day after the first article appeared, Nixon's chief of staff, H. R. "Bob" Haldeman, explained just how damaging the papers might be. Not only did the Pentagon Papers have the potential to turn public opinion against the war, which is eventually what happened, the documents could undermine Nixon's presidency. According to a tape made of a conversation between Haldeman and Nixon on June 14, 1971, Haldeman quoted White House aide Donald Rumsfeld, saying, "To the ordinary guy, all this is a bunch of gobbledygook. But out of the gobbledygook comes a very clear thing: you can't trust the government; you can't believe what they say; and you can't rely on their judgment. And the implicit infallibility of presidents, which has been an accepted thing in

America, is badly hurt by this, because it shows that people do things the president wants to do even though it's wrong, and the president can be wrong."[1]

As soon as the first *New York Times* article appeared, Ellsberg and his wife went into hiding. Nixon demanded the source of the leak be found, and it didn't take the FBI long to identify Ellsberg. Under increasing pressure from the White House to locate him, federal agents conducted what was reported to be the largest manhunt since the kidnapping of Charles Lindbergh's baby.

On June 28, Ellsberg turned himself in to the U.S. Attorney in Boston, Massachusetts. He was arrested and charged with 12 felonies, including theft, conspiracy, and espionage. If convicted on all counts, he could receive 115 years in jail. But Nixon wanted more—he wanted to prevent any more leaks. To accomplish that, the Special Investigation Unit was formed.

The Plumbers included E. Howard Hunt, a former CIA operative, and G. Gordon Liddy, an ex-FBI agent. John Paisley, Director of the CIA's Office of Security, was the agency's go-between with the Plumbers. Because of Paisley's involvement, it was later concluded that the CIA was not only aware of the Plumbers' illegal operations, but quite probably assisted in the planning of them. Curiously, the connection was never officially investigated.

The group was headed by Egil Krogh, who at the time was the White House Deputy for Domestic Affairs. Ironically, Krogh had the reputation for being a straight arrow, hardly the type of loose cannon one would expect to be running the President's Dirty Tricks squad. But Krogh believed what he was doing was in the interest of national security.

"At the time, the atmosphere was one of extreme concern over what the president viewed as a major security breakdown," Krogh said in a 2002 interview with Bill Straub. "He felt under attack from within. Top-secret documents were being disclosed at a pace far beyond any-

thing we had seen in the past. If it continued, our ability to carry out Vietnam would be seriously compromised.

"I think there was an idea among some of us that the president's constitutional authority as commander in chief would justify certain types of actions that were beyond the law."[2]

In other words, Nixon believed certain laws did not apply to him because he was President.

Around the time the Plumbers were being organized, a memo was sent from Nixon's chief lawyer, Chuck Colson, outlining a Political Enemies Project and listing the enemies. Among those listed were football star Joe Namath, actor Paul Newman, the editor of the *Los Angeles Times,* and CBS reporter Daniel Schorr. Later, White House attorney John Dean explained that the purpose of the project was to see "how we can use the available federal machinery to screw our political enemies," such as having the Internal Revenue Service audit people on the list.[3]

Meanwhile, the Plumbers were preparing for their first mission. Krogh organized a plan to break in to the Beverly Hills office of Ellsberg's psychiatrist Lewis J. Fielding. They hoped to find personal information in Ellsberg's medical file that might discredit him or perhaps even drive him to suicide if it were made public. The assignment was carried out by E. Howard Hunt and G. Gordon Liddy in September 1971. They were unable to locate the file.

Afterward, Nixon's assistant for domestic affairs, John Ehrlichman, told the President, "We had one little operation. It's been aborted out in Los Angeles which, I think, is better that you don't know about."[4]

The most brazen and shocking plan was to physically assault Ellsberg. On May 3, 1972, a dozen Cubans who worked with the CIA were flown to Washington, D.C., with orders to "incapacitate" Ellsberg by literally breaking his legs. The recruits had to abort the plan because there were too many people around Ellsberg.

John Ehrlichman was Nixon's domestic affairs adviser. He was involved in the cover-up from the beginning.

Ehrlichman resigned, hoping to protect the President from further scrutiny. He was convicted of obstruction of justice, conspiracy, and perjury, for lying under oath to a Senate committee about the break-in at Daniel Ellsberg's doctor's Beverly Hills office. He died in 1999 of complications from diabetes.

The Plumbers appeared to be veering out of control, but by that time Krogh had left the White House. After objecting to some of the people who were being wiretapped, he resigned and moved to St. Louis. Liddy was reassigned to work for CREEP and brought Hunt with him.

Liddy asked Attorney General John Mitchell for $1 million to bankroll Operation Gemstone, his code name for what would be a series of missions carried out against Nixon's political enemies. Mitchell agreed to give Liddy $250,000 for a less ambitious "intelligence gathering" plan. Top on his list was to bug the offices of the DNC. It was Liddy who recruited McCord and the others to break into the Watergate offices. What nobody planned on was getting caught.

Krogh says that when he read about the break-in and saw the names of the men arrested, "I knew it was only a matter of time before all the previous incidents became exposed."[5]

From the beginning, reporters Bob Woodward and Carl Bernstein sensed the Watergate break-in was much more than what White House Press Secretary Ron Ziegler dismissed as a "third-rate burglary." They set out to see just how high the government's involvement went.

The first link to the White House was the discovery of E. Howard Hunt's phone number in one of the burglars' notebooks. Then a friend of Woodward who worked in the government tipped him off that some of Nixon's top aides had paid the burglars to dig up dirt on his political opponents. Working off that lead, by August the reporters had linked the burglars to CREEP. They had followed the money—a $25,000 cashier's check intended for the Nixon campaign had been deposited into the bank account of a Watergate burglar. The trail led to Attorney General John Mitchell, who controlled the CREEP funds.

If it hadn't been for Carl Bernstein (left) and Bob Woodward, the truth about Watergate might have never been known.

With the help of a secret source they named Deep Throat, Woodward and Bernstein slowly helped unravel the Watergate conspiracy and indirectly forced Nixon's resignation from office. They would both receive the Pultizer Prize for journalism.

When Bernstein called Mitchell for a comment, he snapped that *Washington Post* publisher "Katie Graham's gonna get . . . caught in a big fat wringer if that's ever published."[6]

That same month, Nixon told reporters, "No one in the White House staff, no one in this administration, presently employed, was involved in this very bizarre incident."[7]

However, on September 29, 1972, the *Post* published the story of the secret Republican fund being used for intelligence gathering against the Democrats. On October 10, Woodward and Bernstein got more specific, reporting that the spying was being done directly on behalf of CREEP.

Much of their information was being supplied by a shadowy, mysterious source Woodward and Bernstein referred to only as Deep Throat. The source held an important job in the government and willingly supplied information on the illegal activities being conducted on behalf of Nixon's administration. It was Deep Throat who first hinted that people at the very highest levels of the White House were involved—even the President himself—in all sorts of illegal activities, including "bugging, following people, false press leaks, fake letters, canceling campaign rallies, investigations of campaign workers' private lives, planting spies, stealing documents, planting provocateurs in political demonstrations."[8]

Despite the dramatic implication of the revelations, on November 7 Nixon was reelected over George McGovern by one of the largest landslides in U.S. history. It would prove to be his last political victory.

It is often true that investigative journalists are only as good as their sources. That Woodward and Bernstein were able to break so many exclusive stories about the Watergate scandal was in large measure due to the mysterious Deep Throat. This person was so highly placed in government that even after Nixon's resignation, the reporters promised to keep the source's identity a secret, literally to the death.

After thirty years of secrecy, in a July 2005 *Vanity Fair* article, W. Mark Felt, the former Associate Director of the FBI, revealed himself to be Deep Throat. As the bureau's number two man, he had been privy to many of the goings-on in the Nixon White House. Although not friends, Felt would often agree to talk to Woodward on various stories as long as his identity was never mentioned. Even before Watergate, Felt had passed along information to Woodward, such as when Vice President Spiro Agnew took a bribe. Two years later, that news would be made public as part of an investigation into Agnew's finances.

W. Mark Felt

When George Wallace was shot, Felt gave Woodward inside FBI information on Arthur H. Bremer, Wallace's would-be assassin, including the fact that he had stalked several candidates. That helped Woodward write several front-page stories, which in turn increased Woodward's reputation as a journalist. Having proven his accuracy and value as a source, one of the first calls Woodward made after being assigned to cover the DNC break-in was to Mark Felt, thus beginning Felt's role as Deep Throat.

As to why Felt, who didn't reveal himself until he was ninety-one and in failing health, agreed to cooperate as extensively as he did on Watergate, Woodward believes Felt was simply determined to protect the FBI from becoming another Dirty Tricks squad for Nixon. "He had nothing but contempt for the Nixon White House and their efforts to manipulate the bureau for political reasons," Woodward said. "The young eager-beaver patrol of White House underlings, best exemplified by John W. Dean III, was odious to him."[8]

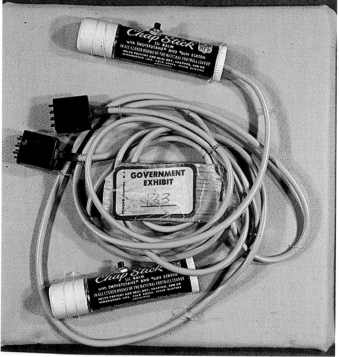

These Chap Stick tubes with hidden microphones were found on the Watergate Hotel burglars. Nixon also used hidden microphones in the Oval Office to record his conversations there.

Between 1940 and 1973, six presidents from both parties had occasionally used this practice. In Nixon's case, the tape recordings were overseen by the Secret Service. Only the President and a few of his top advisers were aware of the tapes' existence. The information on those tapes would ultimately end Nixon's presidency.

CHAPTER 4

"A Cancer on the Presidency"

On January 8, 1973, the five Watergate burglars, along with G. Gordon Liddy and E. Howard Hunt, went on trial. Within the week, Hunt, Barker, Gonzalez, Martinez, and Sturgis pled guilty. The presiding judge, John J. Sirica, was so incredulous that they had acted independently that he actually questioned the defendants himself outside the presence of the jury, a highly unusual thing for a judge to do. At the time, they all held firm to their story.

Liddy and McCord, who had pled not guilty, were convicted of conspiracy, burglary, and wiretapping on January 30.

Although several of his former aides had been convicted of the crime, Nixon continued to deny any knowledge of or involvement in the Watergate break-in. On February 7 the Senate voted unanimously to convene the Select Committee on Presidential Campaign Activities, also known as the Senate Watergate Committee. Its task was to investigate the allegations of political spying and sabotage conducted on behalf of Nixon and his reelection campaign. The committee was a bipartisan panel of seven senators: Sam Ervin (D), Howard Baker (R), Ed Gurney (R), Daniel Inouye (D), Joseph Montoya (D), Herman Talmadge (D), and Lowell Weicker, Jr. (R).

Then came the first of many bombshells in the case—in March James McCord wrote a letter to Judge Sirica. In it he admitted that he and his fellow defendants had lied under oath and the truth was, higher-ups *had* ordered the break-in and that he and his co-defendants pled guilty under great pressure from both John Dean, one of the Nixon

administration attorneys, and John Mitchell, the Attorney General. Woodward and Bernstein would reveal in their book *All the President's Men* that McCord was told by another of Nixon's Dirty Tricks henchmen, Jack Caulfield, "Your life is no good in this country if you don't cooperate."[1]

McCord might have never written the letter had Nixon not fired CIA chief Richard Helms in February 1973. As director of the U.S. spy agency, Helms had agreed to what was called the Houston Plan and spy on American citizens for Nixon—even though it is illegal for the CIA to operate within the United States and target its citizens. But Helms and Nixon had a falling out after the President tried to force Helms to pay hush money to E. Howard Hunt, who was threatening to go public with the truth about the Plumbers. When Helms refused, Nixon fired him.

That upset McCord so much, he decided to come forward. Sirica immediately contacted Senator Sam Ervin, who was chairman of the Watergate Committee. In an official statement made to Ervin, McCord outlined many of the activities of Liddy's Operation Gemstone.

Once McCord came forward, events moved so fast hardly a day, much less week, went by without a new shocking revelation. In early April, John Dean began cooperating with the Watergate prosecutors. On April 30, Nixon went on television to address the nation, announcing he had fired John Dean and had accepted the resignations of Ehrlichman and Haldeman.

In his speech, Nixon maintained he was shocked to learn that "some of my closest friends and most trusted aides have been charged with involvement in what has come to be known as the Watergate affair." Although, as he said, he couldn't believe anyone in his administration would ever be involved in anything illegal, Nixon continued, "However, new information then came to me which persuaded me that there was a real possibility that some of these charges were true, and suggesting further that there had been an effort to conceal the facts both from the public, from you, and from me."

Unlike the others involved in the burglary, McCord refused to plead guilty. After his conviction, he supplied valuable information to Judge John Sirica that helped uncover the truth about Nixon's illegal activities.

James McCord was a former FBI agent and CIA operative.

Stressing his innocence, he added, "On March 21, I personally assumed the responsibility for coordinating intensive new inquiries into the matter, and I personally ordered those conducting the investigations to get all the facts and to report them directly to me, right here in this office."[2]

To borrow a phrase, that was like having the fox guard the henhouse.

On May 18, Archibald Cox was appointed Special Prosecutor for Watergate. That same day, the committee's hearings began and were televised gavel to gavel until it concluded on August 7. At the time, there were only three national broadcast networks—NBC, ABC, and CBS—as well as the publicly funded PBS. The three main networks took turns

and rotated the live coverage. At night, PBS would play a tape of that day's testimony.

The only time all three networks carried live coverage simultaneously was for John Dean's thirty hours of testimony, which began June 25. The country was riveted—and stunned—as he outlined in excruciating detail Nixon's involvement in the cover-up. In one of the most famous moments of the hearings, Dean recalled, "I began by telling the President there was a cancer growing on the presidency, and if the cancer was not removed, the President himself would be killed by it."[3]

Dean's testimony was compelling, believable, and damning. Nixon became combative, declining to appear before the committee and refusing to give access to any presidential documents. He claimed he didn't have to because of Executive Privilege, which is the belief that the President and other top executives have the right to withhold confidential information from the courts or even Congress.

That argument was about to be put to a severe test when a former Nixon secretary, Alexander P. Butterfield, mentioned during a pretestimony interview that the President routinely tape-recorded all his telephone calls and conversations. In his office, there were five microphones in his desk and two by the fireplace. There were more placed in the Cabinet room and even at the Presidential Retreat in Camp David.

The news was explosive. Suddenly, it wasn't just John Dean's word against the President's. Butterfield had revealed a way to prove—beyond any doubt—Dean's accusations. It would also start one of the bitterest, and most important, legal battles in U.S. history.

Special Prosecutor Cox demanded Nixon immediately turn over all tapes, along with other documents. Nixon refused. The Watergate Committee obtained a subpoena, which is an order from a judge to comply with the request. Nixon again refused, and in another national address, cited Executive Privilege:

> Each day, a President of the United States is required to make difficult decisions on grave issues. It is absolutely

necessary, if the President is to be able to do his job as the country expects, that he be able to talk openly and candidly with his advisers about issues and individuals. This kind of frank discussion is only possible when those who take part in it know that what they say is in strictest confidence. . . .

That is why I shall continue to oppose efforts which would set a precedent that would cripple all future Presidents by inhibiting conversations between them and those they look to for advice. . . .

This principle of confidentiality of Presidential conversations is at stake in the question of these tapes. I must and I shall oppose any efforts to destroy this principle, which is so vital to the conduct of this great office.[4]

The Senate committee didn't buy it. As Senator Baker put it, "The central question is simply put—what did the president know and when did he know it?"[5]

Judge Sirica wondered the same thing. On August 29, 1973, he ordered Nixon to turn over nine tapes relevant to Watergate for the judge to review privately, eliminating the possibility that unrelated confidential information would be made public. Nixon again refused and appealed the ruling to the U.S. Circuit Court of Appeals.

On October 12 the Court of Appeals upheld Judge Sirica's ruling. A week later, Nixon offered a compromise, suggesting that Senator John Stennis review the tapes and present Cox with summaries. On October 20, the Special Prosecutor officially refused the compromise. That evening, millions of Americans sat home watching what was then one of the most popular nights of television. Just as *All in the Family* ended on the East Coast, regular programming was interrupted. In what would become known as the Saturday Night Massacre, stunned reporters went on the air to announce that Nixon just had Archibald Cox "fired" and abolished the office of the Special Prosecutor.

Nixon offered to let Stennis listen to the tapes, assuming it would be easier to skirt by the senator than the prosecutor. When Cox refused the compromise, Nixon abolished the office of the Special Prosecutor, setting off a Constitutional crisis.

John Stennis from Mississippi served in the U.S. Senate for 42 years, from 1947 to 1989.

The President had originally ordered Attorney General Elliot Richardson to fire Cox, but he refused and resigned in protest. Deputy Attorney General William Ruckelshaus also refused the order and was fired by Nixon. Finally, Robert Bork, acting as Attorney General, agreed and fired Cox.

Commenting on Nixon's actions, Cox told reporters, "Whether ours shall continue to be a government of laws and not of men is now for Congress and ultimately the American people."[6]

Suddenly Watergate wasn't just about a break-in and spying; it had become a test to see if our very Constitution would survive.

The Mary Tyler Moore Show

The cast of the
Mary Tyler Moore Show

CBS's Saturday comedy lineup for the 1973–74 television season is now considered legendary. When news of the Saturday Night Massacre interrupted regular programming, more people than ever before or since were staying home on Saturday nights to watch *All in the Family*, *M*A*S*H*, *The Mary Tyler Moore Show*, *The Bob Newhart Show*, and *The Carol Burnett Show*.

Perhaps no show reflected the changing of American culture more than *The Mary Tyler Moore Show*. When the show premiered in September 1970, it was one of the first sitcoms to feature a single, never-before-married working woman in her thirties whose main preoccupation was her job and coworkers—not finding a husband or having children. It was also one of the first shows in which the men were truly just colleagues and friends and not love interests for the lead actress. While the workplace comedy was not exactly a new premise for sitcoms, it was redefined in *The Mary Tyler Moore Show* because her coworkers at the TV station newsroom became her family.

Although common now, the character of Mary Richards was breaking important new television ground and resonated with a generation of women who found themselves in similar situations. While Mary Richards herself wasn't portrayed as a feminist, the show's depiction of a successful single woman who intends to "make it on her own" is credited for advancing the cause of equality for women simply because people liked the show and found Mary Richards, and actress Mary Tyler Moore, non-threatening.

The show skillfully alternated between humor grounded in real life and complete silliness. One of the most famous episodes was when Chuckles the Clown was accidentally crushed to death by an elephant while he's dressed as Peter Peanut. Mary is appalled that her coworkers can make jokes about Chuckles' untimely death and chastises them. It's not until the middle of the funeral when Mary is finally struck by the absurdity of it and begins laughing inappropriately—and uncontrollably.

When Moore and her husband Grant Tinker, who was also the show's executive producer, decided to end the show and go out on top, they were among the first to produce a "series finale" episode to bring the show to closure. In the last episode, the station is sold and the new owner fires everyone but the incompetent anchor Ted Baxter, played by Ted Knight. In the final scene, the cast of regulars share a group hug before Mary returns for one final look at the newsroom, switches off the light, and closes the door.

THE WHITE HOUSE
WASHINGTON

August 9, 1974

Dear Mr. Secretary:

I hereby resign the Office of President of the
United States.

Sincerely,

Richard N

The Honorable Henry A. Kissinger
The Secretary of State
Washington, D. C. 20520

With eleven words, Richard Nixon became the only president in American history to resign.

Nixon's presidency would forever change the way Americans looked at—and trusted—politicians. It was a reminder to citizens of the importance of a free press, the necessity of checks and balances within government, and the dangers of absolute power.

Disgrace

The fallout from the Saturday Night Massacre was immediate. Over the following week outraged citizens flooded the White House with almost a half million angry telegrams. For the first time, members of Congress began to speak openly of impeaching the President, with several members already prepared to start drafting the Articles of Impeachment.

Impeachment is the two-step process by which Congress may remove a high-ranking government official, such as a President, Vice President or Supreme Court Justice, from office for "treason, bribery, or other high crimes and misdemeanors." First, the House of Representatives must present the charges. Then the Senate conducts a trial. A two-thirds majority is needed to convict. If found guilty, the official is removed from office.

Facing extreme pressure from both the public and Congress, Nixon finally relented and agreed to turn over selected tapes to the new Special Prosecutor, Leon Jaworski, who had been appointed by the Justice Department.

Still defiant, Nixon continued to maintain his innocence. On November 17, he appeared at an Associated Press event in Florida. At one point during the heated question-and-answer period, Nixon vehemently denied the accusations being leveled against him and defended his fight against turning over the tapes.

"In all of my years of public life, I have never obstructed justice," Nixon claimed. "And I think, too, that I should say that in my

years of public life that I've welcomed this kind of examination, because people have got to know whether or not their President's a crook. Well, I'm not a crook!"[1]

The comment became the butt of jokes, because just four days later when the tapes were finally turned over, two were missing and others had suspicious gaps of silence. An electronics expert concluded that one particular eighteen-minute gap—originally recorded just three days after the Watergate break-in—was the result of five separate erasures, meaning the gap was intentional and not accidental.

For the next five months, Nixon and Jaworski continued to wage a legal battle over the tapes. As the months passed, more and more people began calling for Nixon's impeachment.

In March, John Ehrlichman, H. R. Haldeman, former Attorney General John Mitchell, and several other former and current members of Nixon's administration were indicted, or charged with crimes, by a federal grand jury. Nixon was also named a coconspirator but was not officially charged. After the indictment was handed down, Jaworski subpoenaed more tapes as evidence in the case he was building against the defendants.

Still desperately fighting to keep the tapes from becoming public, Nixon instead gave the Special Prosecutor over 1,000 pages of tape transcripts, claiming the document proved his innocence. The public got quite a different impression. Many were shocked at his liberal use of profanity. There were so many places where swear words had been replaced with "expletive deleted" that the phrase became part of pop culture, in the same way "The tribe has spoken" and "You're fired" became catch phrases in the early 2000s.

Beyond the language, it was Nixon's demeanor that painted the picture of a paranoid, dangerous leader. As *Washington Post* reporter George Lardner noted in 1997:

> On the tapes, Nixon is profane, demanding, delighted, sad, insightful, angry, exultant, calculating and bitter. . . .

If there is one guiding principle about Nixon that stands out on these tapes, it is this: Do unto others what you think they have done unto you. . . .

They show Nixon demanding a break-in at the Brookings Institution, relishing the idea of a chance to "blackmail" Lyndon Johnson, anticipating a cascade of money from International Telephone & Telegraph Co. in return for an antitrust settlement, chortling at the idea of planting a spy or two in the Secret Service detail assigned to Sen. Edward M. Kennedy in 1972.

"We just might get lucky and catch this son of a bitch," Nixon says of Kennedy. "Ruin him for '76. . . . It's going to be fun."[2]

The tug-of-war over the tapes finally reached the Supreme Court. On July 24, in front of a packed room, Chief Justice Warren E. Burger read the unanimous decision that the tapes subpoenaed by Jaworski must immediately be turned over to the Special Prosecutor and that Nixon "must yield to the demonstrated, specific need for evidence in a pending criminal trial,"[3] rejecting the Executive Privilege argument.

Washington Post reporter John Mackenzie noted, "Only a few times in its history has the court grappled with such large assertions of governmental power. As in most of those encounters, the justices concluded that the judiciary must have the last word in an orderly constitutional system."[4]

Nixon knew he had finally run out of time. If he didn't turn over the tapes, he would be impeached for defying the Supreme Court. But by turning over the tapes, he provided Jaworski with the smoking gun— incontrovertible proof that Nixon was part of the cover-up by trying to prevent the FBI from investigating the break-in.

In a conversation that took place on June 23, 1972, Nixon orders Haldeman to "call the FBI and say that we wish, for the country, don't go any further into this case, period."[5]

The House passed three articles of impeachment:

RESOLVED, That Richard M. Nixon, President of the United States, is impeached for high crimes and misdemeanors, and that the following articles of impeachment to be exhibited to the Senate:

Article 1: Obstruction of Justice.

Article 2: Abuse of Power.

Article 3: Contempt of Congress.[6]

There was little doubt that Nixon would be found guilty in a Senate trial. Rather than further taint the office of the president, Congress accepted Nixon's resignation. On August 9, 1974, Richard Nixon became the first president of the United States to resign from office. Even as Gerald Ford was being sworn in as President, Jaworski was recommending that Nixon be prosecuted.

Although twenty-five people would eventually be convicted of crimes stemming from Nixon's activities as President, Nixon himself was not one of them. In a controversial move that outraged many citizens, Ford gave Nixon an executive pardon, meaning Nixon could never be prosecuted for any crimes committed while he had been president.

Among the reasons Ford gave for his decision was the concern that Nixon would never get a fair trial, that he and his family had suffered enough already, and that pardoning him was in the best interest of the country. He asserted, "During this long period of delay and potential litigation, ugly passions would again be aroused. And our people would again be polarized in their opinions. And the credibility of our free institutions of government would again be challenged at home and abroad."[7]

Although many disagreed with Ford's decision, everyone agreed that Nixon and the Watergate scandal forever changed the way Americans view and trust their leaders.

He was appointed vice president by Nixon, with Congressional approval, after Spiro Agnew resigned. Ford became president when Nixon was forced to resign. Many historians believe Ford lost the 1976 election over lingering resentment that he had pardoned Nixon.

Gerald Ford is the only president not to have been elected as either vice president or president.

Sam Ervin, who led the Senate Watergate Committee, called it "the greatest tragedy this country has ever suffered. I used to think that the Civil War was our country's greatest tragedy, but I do remember that there were some redeeming features in the Civil War in that there was some spirit of sacrifice and heroism displayed on both sides. I see no redeeming features in Watergate."[8]

FYInfo
FOR YOUR INFORMATION

Andrew Johnson

Prior to Nixon, only one other American president had faced impeachment proceedings. In 1868 the U.S. Senate put Andrew Johnson on trial in the aftermath of the Civil war. Just as with Nixon, there were people who felt Johnson was abusing the power of his office, while others believed him to be the victim of unfair, partisan politics.

Unlike the way it is today, with presidential nominees choosing their running mates for vice president, back then members of the political party voted on who *they* thought would be the best vice presidential candidate. Johnson was selected to run with Lincoln during his second term in part because he came from Tennessee, a move intended to show that "loyal" Southerners were still welcome to be part of American government.

After Lincoln died on April 15, 1865, Johnson became the 17th President of the United States, and his troubles began almost immediately. The Civil War had been over for less than a week, and there was already heated debate in Congress about what procedures Southern states should have to go through to be readmitted into the Union, and whether each state had the right to establish its own policies regarding former slaves.

In early 1866, Johnson vetoed the Civil Rights Act, which would have guaranteed all blacks in all American states the rights of citizenship, such as voting and being allowed to own property. This infuriated supporters of Lincoln in the Congress. Johnson's veto was overturned—the first time in U.S. history a presidential veto of a major piece of legislation was overridden. From there, things quickly went downhill for Johnson, with his fiercest opponents—known as the Radical Republicans—calling him an outlaw. His outspoken opposition to the proposed 14th Amendment, which would guarantee equal protection and due process for all citizens, didn't help.

In February 1868, Johnson dismissed Edwin Stanton—who had served under Lincoln and was sympathetic to the black cause—as his Secretary of War and replaced him with Lorenzo Thomas. The problem was, a law in effect at the time called the Tenure of Office Act forbade the President to replace any Cabinet member without the approval of Congress. Johnson broke the law, hoping to force the Supreme Court to rule whether the act was constitutional or not. Instead, three days later the House of Representatives agreed to impeach him for high crimes and misdemeanors.

The trial began in late March 1868 and lasted almost two months. On May 16, the Senate voted. A two-thirds majority was needed to impeach Johnson. The final tally was 35-19 against Johnson—he had been acquitted by one vote.

Chronology

1968
November   Richard Milhous Nixon defeats Hubert Humphrey for the presidency

1972
June 17   Burglars apprehended at DNC offices at the Watergate Hotel
November 7   Nixon elected to second term as U.S. President

1973
February 7   Senate Watergate Committee formed to investigate the burglary
April 30   Chief of Staff H. R. Haldeman and adviser John Ehrlichman are forced to resign; White House counsel John Dean is fired
May 18   Archibald Cox is named Special Prosecutor
June 25–29   John Dean implicates Nixon in cover-up
July 23   Nixon refuses to turn over the White House tapes
October 10   Vice President Spiro T. Agnew resigns after being charged with tax evasion
October 12   Nixon nominates Gerald Ford to replace Agnew
October 20   Saturday Night Massacre: Nixon fires Archibald Cox and abolishes the Special Prosecutor position; Attorney General Elliot Richardson and Deputy Attorney General William Ruckelshaus also lose their jobs
November 1   The Justice Department names Leon Jaworski new Special Prosecutor
November 17   Nixon makes his famous "I'm not a crook" speech

1974
April 11   House of Representatives subpoenas Nixon's secret tapes
July 24   Supreme Court rules Nixon must turn over secret tapes
July 27   Senate Judiciary Committee passes Article of Impeachment
August 9   Nixon resigns; Gerald Ford is sworn in as President
September 8   Ford pardons Nixon

1994
April 22   Richard Nixon dies in California at the age of 81

2005
May 31   W. Mark Felt reveals himself to be Deep Throat

Timeline in History

1929   Former Secretary of the Interior Albert Fall is convicted of bribery stemming from when Fall secretly leased the government-owned Teapot Dome petroleum reserve to private developers.

1935   Louisiana Senator Huey Long is assassinated.

1951   British spies for the Soviet Union Guy Burgess and Donald Maclean flee to Russia.

1961   President John Kennedy okays Bay of Pigs invasion, an attempt to overthrow Cuba's leader Fidel Castro.

1963   Governor of Alabama George Wallace bars two black students from enrolling at the University of Alabama.

1975   America withdraws from Vietnam.

1978   The FBI initiates Abscam, an undercover operation that eventually results in the conviction of four U.S. Representatives and one U.S. Senator for bribery.

1984   Geraldine Ferraro becomes the first female candidate on a major ticket for vice president.

1986   In the Iran-Contra Affair, money from the sale of weapons to Iran is given to Nicaraguan rebels to overthrow the government.

1990   Washington, D.C., mayor Marion Barry is arrested on drug charges.

1998   President Bill Clinton is impeached for lying about his relationship with Monica Lewinsky.

2001   Enron files for bankruptcy and is accused of manipulating the California energy crisis.

2002   U.S. Representative James Traficant is found guilt of bribery and racketeering.

2005   The 2003 Plame Affair, in which Valerie Plame is identified as a CIA operative, results in the jailing of journalist Judith Miller for refusing to identify her sources without their consent.

2006   Tom DeLay officially steps down as House Majority leader while waiting trial on conspiracy and money laundering charges. President George W. Bush faces disciplinary action for authorizing the National Security Agency to wiretap Americans suspected of links to terrorism without a court warrant.

Chapter Notes

Chapter 1 In the Dead of the Night

1. Alfred E. Lewis, "5 Held in Plot to Bug Democrats' Office Here," *The Washington Post*, June 18, 1972, p. A1, 2, http://www.washingtonpost.com/wp-srv/national/longterm/watergate/articles/061972-1.htm.

2. Carl Bernstein and Bob Woodward, "GOP Security Aide Among Five Arrested in Bugging Affair," *The Washington Post*, June 19, 1972, p. A01, http://www.washingtonpost.com/wp-srv/local/longterm/tours/scandal/watergat.htm.

3. Ibid.

4. Ibid.

5. William Raspberry, "The 'Watergate Hero,' " *The Washington Post*, November 6, 1973, p. A23.

6. John Aloysius Farrell, "Watergate's Hero Forgotten, Alone Former Guard Broods in a Cabin in the Woods," *Boston Globe*, June 15, 1997, p. A2.

Chapter 2 The Seeds of Paranoia

1. PBS, "Nixon's China Game," http://www.pbs.org/wgbh/amex/china/peopleevents/pande01.html.

Chapter 3 Accusations

1. World Crisis Web, Truths Worth Telling, http://www.world-crisis.com/analysis_comments/822_0_15_0_C38.

2. Bill Straub, "Leader of Nixon's 'Plumbers' Regrets Loss of Integrity," Scripps Howard News Service, Saturday, June 15, 2002, http://seattlepi.nwsource.com/national/74766_watergate15.shtml.

3. *Newshour* Transcript: Nixon Tapes, November 27, 1997; transcript of tape from September 8, 1971, http://www.pbs.org/newshour/bb/white_house/july-dec97/nixon_11-26.html.

4. Straub.

5. *Washington Post*. Revisiting Watergate, Key Players: John Mitchell, http://www.washingtonpost.com/wp-srv/onpolitics/watergate/Johnmitchell.html.

6. Carl Bernstein and Bob Woodward, "Dean Alleges Nixon Knew of Cover-up Plan," *Washington Post*, Sunday, June 3, 1973, p. A01, http://www.washingtonpost.com/wp-dyn/content/article/2002/05/31/AR2005112200792.html.

7. Bob Woodward and Carl Bernstein, *All the President's Men* (New York: Simon & Schuster, 1994), pp. 134–135.

8. Bob Woodward, "How Mark Felt Became 'Deep Throat,' " *Washington Post*, June 2, 2005, p. A01, http://www.washingtonpost.com/wp-dyn/content/article/2005/06/01/AR2005060102124_5.html.

Chapter 4 "A Cancer on the Presidency"

1. Bob Woodward and Carl Bernstein, *All the President's Men* (New York: Simon & Schuster, 1994), p. 318.

2. Nixon's First Watergate Speech, April 30, 1973, http://www.watergate.info/nixon/73-04-30watergate-speech.shtml.

3. *NOW with Bill Moyers*, transcript from April 2, 2004, http://www.pbs.org/now/transcript/transcript314_full.html.

4. Nixon's Second Watergate Speech, August 15, 1973, http://www.watergate.info/nixon/73-08-15watergate-speech.shtml.

5. BBC News, "Echoes of Nixon," December 2, 1998, http://news.bbc.co.uk/1/hi/events/clinton_under_fire/the_big_picture/226538.stm.

6. Carroll Kilpatrick, "Nixon Forces Firing of Cox; Richardson, Ruckelshaus Quit; President Abolishes Prosecutor's Office; FBI Seals Records," *Washington Post*, October 21, 1973, p. A01, http://www.washingtonpost.com/wp-dyn/content/article/2002/06/03/AR2005112200799.html.

Chapter 5 Disgrace

1. Watergate Chronology, 1973, http://www.watergate.info/chronology/1973.shtml.

2. George Lardner Jr., "Behind the Statesman, A Reel Nixon Endures," *Washington Post*, June 17, 1997, p. A01, http://www.washingtonpost.com/wp-dyn/content/article/2002/06/11/AR2005112200812.html.

3. John P. MacKenzie, "Court Orders Nixon to Yield Tapes; President Promises to Comply Fully," *Washington Post*, July 25, 1974, p. A01, http://www.washingtonpost.com/wp-dyn/content/article/2002/06/03/AR2005112200805.html.

4. Ibid.

5. The History Place—Sounds of History "A secret recording of President Nixon telling top aide H.R. Haldeman to obstruct the FBI investigation into the Watergate break-in, June 23, 1972," http://www.historyplace.com/specials/sounds-prez/.

6. The History Place—Presidential Impeachment Proceedings, "Richard M. Nixon, 37th U.S. President," http://www.historyplace.com/unitedstates/impeachments/nixon.htm.

7. "President Gerald R. Ford's Remarks on Signing a Proclamation Granting Pardon to Richard Nixon," September 8, 1974, http://www.ford.utexas.edu/library/speeches/740060.htm.

8. Carroll Kilpatrick, "President Refuses to Turn Over Tapes; Ervin Committee, Cox Issue Subpoenas; Action Sets Stage for Court Battle on Powers Issue," *Washington Post*, July 24, 1973, p. A01, http://www.washingtonpost.com/wp-dyn/content/article/2002/06/03/AR2005112200796.html.

Glossary

audit (AW-dit)
To closely examine a person's or organization's finances.

bipartisan (bye-PAR-teh-zin)
Involving people from two political parties, such as Democrats and Republicans.

bug
To wiretap a room or a phone.

extricating (EK-strih-kay-ting)
Untangling and freeing something.

Executive Privilege (egg-ZECK-kyoo-tiv PRIV-lej)
The claim that a president has the right to withhold documents from a court.

impeach (im-PEECH)
To bring charges against a government official by the legislature.

paranoia (pair-uh-NOY-uh)
The fear that you are being unfairly persecuted.

partisan (PAR-teh-zin)
A passionate belief in a particular party, cause, or agenda.

perjury (PUR-juh-ree)
To lie when under oath in a court.

prosecutor (PRAH-seh-kyoo-tur)
An attorney who prosecutes criminals on behalf of a state or country.

provocateur (proe-vah-kuh-TER)
Anyone who purposely stirs others into action.

subpoenaed (suh-PEE-nud)
Ordered by the court, in writing, to appear before the court or to produce documents or other evidence to the court.

Further Reading

For Young Adults

Cohen, Daniel. *Watergate: Deception in the White House.* Spotlight on American History. Brookfield, CT: The Millbrook Press, 1998.

Fremon, David K. *The Watergate Scandal in American History.* Berkeley Heights, NJ: Enslow Publishers, 1998.

Hargrove, Jim. *The Story of Watergate.* Cornerstones of Freedom. New York: Children's Press, 1989.

Herda, D. J. *United States v. Nixon: Watergate and the President.* Landmark Supreme Court Cases. Berkeley Heights, NJ: Enslow Publishers, 1996.

Works Consulted

Bernstein, Carl, and Bob Woodward. "GOP Security Aide Among Five Arrested in Bugging Affair," *The Washington Post,* June 19, 1972, p. A01.

Bernstein, Carl, and Bob Woodward, "Dean Alleges Nixon Knew of Cover-up Plan," *The Washington Post,* June 3, 1973, p. A01.

Farrell, John Aloysius. "Watergate's Hero Forgotten, Alone: Former Guard Broods in a Cabin in the Woods," *Boston Globe,* June 15, 1997, p. A2.

Lewis, Alfred E. "5 Held in Plot to Bug Democrats' Office Here," *The Washington Post,* June 18, 1972, pp. A1, 2.

Raspberry, William. "The 'Watergate Hero,'" *The Washington Post,* November 6, 1973, p. A23.

Straub, Bill. "Leader of Nixon's 'Plumbers' Regrets Loss of Integrity," *Scripps Howard News Service,* June 15, 2002.

Woodward, Bob. "How Mark Felt Became 'Deep Throat,' " *Washington Post,* June 2, 2005, p. A01.

Woodward, Bob and Carl Bernstein. *All the President's Men.* New York: Simon & Schuster. 1994.

On the Internet

BBC News: *The Big Picture,* "Echoes of Nixon"
http://news.bbc.co.uk/1/hi/events/clinton_under_fire/the_big_picture/226538.stm

Cable News Network: *All Politics,* "Watergate Revisited"
http://www.cnn.com/ALLPOLITICS/1997/gen/resources/watergate/

The History Channel: Video & Speeches
http://www.historychannel.com/broadband/home/index.jsp

The Museum of Broadcast Communications: *Watergate*
http://www.museum.tv/archives/etv/W/htmlW/watergate/watergate.htm

The National Security Archive, The Pentagon Papers: Secrets, Lies, and Audiotapes; Nixon Tape transcript from June 14, 1971.
http://www.gwu.edu/~nsarchiv/NSAEBB/NSAEBB48/

Nixon Era Times: *The Official Publication Of the Nixon Era Center at Mountain State University*
http://www.watergate.com

PBS: *Newshour Transcript,* "Nixon Tapes"
http://www.pbs.org/newshour/bb/white_house/july-dec97/nixon_11-26.html

Washington Post: Revisiting Watergate, "The Watergate Story"
http://www.washingtonpost.com/wp-srv/onpolitics/watergate/splash.html

Watergate.info: *The Scandal That Brought Down Richard Nixon*
http://www.watergate.info

Index